# TARA'S TELESCOPE

Mary Rosewald



Infomax Readers

Rosen Classroom™

New York

Published in 2014 by The Rosen Publishing Group, Inc.
29 East 21st Street, New York, NY 10010



Book Design: Mickey Harmon

Photo Credits: Cover roman makhmutov/Flickr/Getty Images; pp. 3, 4, 6, 8, 10, 12, 14, 16, 18, 20, 22–24 (background) Iliveinoctober/Shutterstock.com; p. 5 LAWRENCE MIGDALE/Photo Researchers/Getty Images; p. 7 (girl) Yuri Acurs/Shutterstock.com; p. 7 (main) Patryk Kosmider/Shutterstock.com; p. 9 (mirror) Sergey Karpov/Shutterstock.com; p. 9 (sand) Boltenkoff/Shutterstock.com; p. 11 Aeromass/Shutterstock.com; p. 13 Peter Dazeley/Photographer's Choice/Getty Images; p. 15 (Galileo) Iryna1/Shutterstock.com; p. 17 (large telescope) Germany Feng/Shutterstock.com; p. 17 (small telescope) wizagent/Shutterstock.com; p. 19 Science & Society Picture Library/Contributor/SSPL/Getty Images; p. 21 Stocktrek Images/Thinkstock.com.

ISBN: 978-1-4777-2655-6
6-pack ISBN: 978-1-4777-2656-3

Manufactured in the United States of America

CPSIA Compliance Information: Batch #CS13RC: For further information contact Rosen Publishing, New York, New York at 1-800-237-9932.

# CONTENTS

# A GREAT TOOL

Tara loves to learn about the planets, moons, and stars in our night sky. She already knows a lot about the **constellations**. But she wants to take a closer look at faraway bodies in space. What can she use?

Tara's teacher, Mr. Green, says she can use a telescope. It's a tool that helps people see things by **magnifying** the image. Telescopes make a distant object take up more room on the "screen" of your eye. Before she buys a telescope, Tara wants to learn how they work.

Mr. Green says telescopes are great tools for kids who want to discover new things!

# SCIENCE OF SIGHT

Tara learns that all sight, with or without a telescope, starts with light. Natural light comes from the sun, but people also use fire and lamps to make light when it's dark.

First, light travels in waves from its **source** and hits the surface of objects. Next, the object takes in some of the waves, while other waves are **reflected**. When we look at an object, the reflected light hits our eyes. The eyes send information to the brain, which makes an image of the object.

A major reason we can't see things very far away is because our eyes can't collect enough reflected light from them.

SUN
LIGHT

# REFLECTION

Mr. Green says that there are two kinds of telescopes: reflecting and refracting. Reflecting telescopes work using reflection.

Light is reflected differently from different kinds of surfaces. If a surface is rough, such as sand, then light will bounce off at many different angles. If a surface is perfectly smooth, such as a mirror, light will bounce off at the same angle. When light reflects evenly off of smooth surfaces, you can see your reflection in the surface!

Now Tara understands why she can see herself in a mirror, but not on many other surfaces.

SMOOTH
SURFACE

ROUGH
SURFACE

Mr. Green shows Tara a reflecting telescope in his classroom. It has a long tube and an eyepiece on top. She looks through it and can see a bird that's very far away!

Tara learns that light from an object enters the telescope through an aperture (AP-uhr-chur), or opening at one end. It travels through the tube and hits a **primary** mirror at the other end. The mirror reflects the light to a secondary mirror. Then, the secondary mirror reflects light to the eyepiece lens, which magnifies the image of the object.

Reflecting telescopes are good to use when it's dim or dark. That's because mirrors can collect light even from a dark object.

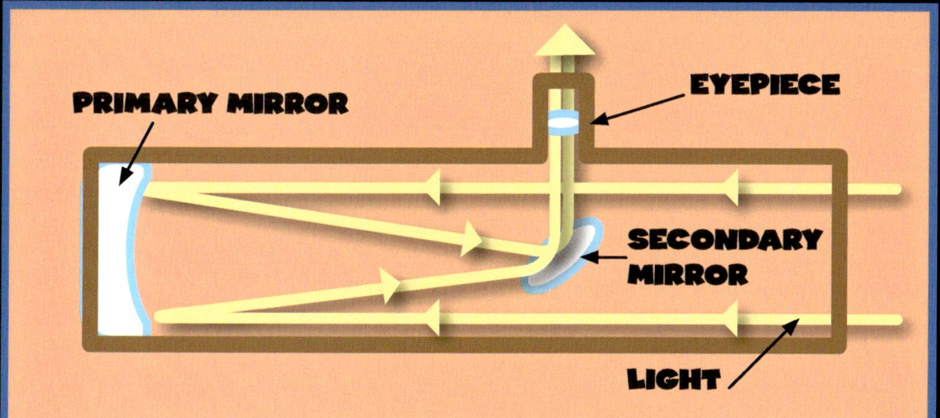


REFLECTING TELESCOPE

# REFRACTION

Tara learns that light is the fastest thing that exists. It travels at different speeds through different mediums, or kinds of matter. For example, it travels very quickly through air, but slows down when it hits water or glass. When light hits the border between two mediums, it seems to "bend," or change direction. This is called refraction.

Refracting telescopes use lenses to bend light a certain way. There are two types of lenses: concave and convex. Concave lenses spread light out, while convex lenses force light to a single point, called a focal point.

Refracting telescopes sometimes use a combination of lenses to magnify an image. Concave lenses curve in, while convex lenses curve out.

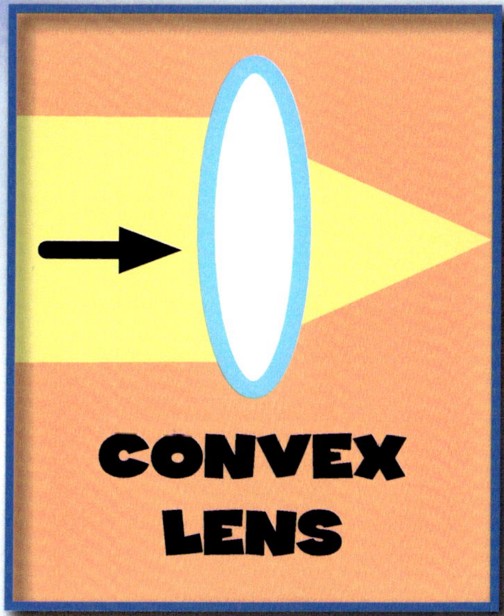
CONVEX
LENS

CONCAVE
LENS

Mr. Green shows Tara a small refracting telescope. He says Hans Lippershey invented this kind of telescope in Holland in 1608. It was the first telescope ever **designed**!

Refracting telescopes use lenses instead of mirrors. Light travels through a primary convex lens in front. This lens focuses the light to a point and sends it to the back of the telescope. Then the light hits another lens at the eyepiece. Lippershey's refracting telescope used convex and concave lenses. Most refracting telescopes today have two convex lenses instead, which make a brighter image.

Galileo was the first person to use a refracting telescope to see things in space. He was an astronomer, or someone who studies things in space.

GALILEO

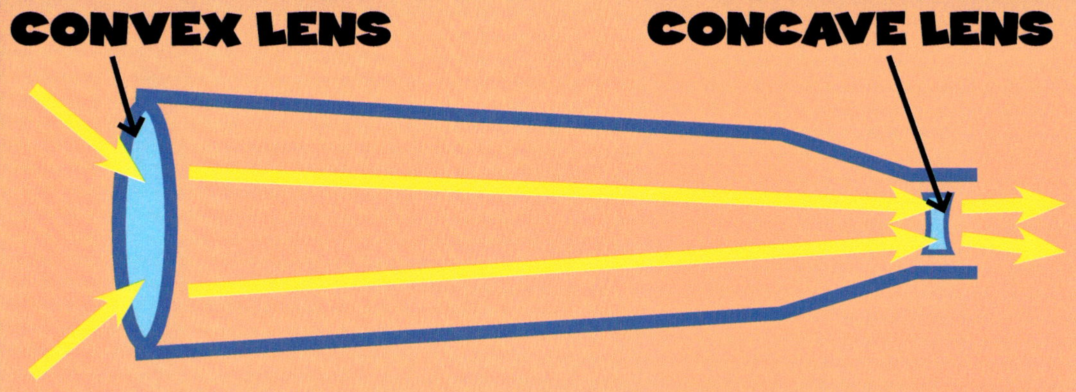


GALILEO'S REFRACTING TELESCOPE

# AT THE STORE

It's time to look for telescopes at the store! Tara asks the salesperson what makes the best telescope. The salesperson says telescopes are judged by how much light they gather and how much they magnify an image.

The amount of light gathered depends on the size of the primary lens or mirror. A big lens or mirror can collect more light. A telescope's magnification depends on the length of the telescope and the length of the eyepiece. A long telescope with a short eyepiece will magnify best.

Tara can buy a small telescope if she wants to see things closer in space or a big telescope to see farther.

# THROUGH A TELESCOPE

Tara's mom buys her a refracting telescope that's just the right size for her. She also buys Tara a book on **stargazing**. It tells her where to look in the night sky to see certain planets, stars, and moons.

First, Tara searches for Saturn and spots its rings. She can't believe she can see a planet that's so far away! Then, she looks at the moon, which usually looks small. With her telescope, she can see many craters she couldn't see before!

Tara also finds Jupiter. It's the biggest planet, so it's not too hard to find. She can even see its four largest moons!

Tara's mom says it's easier to see objects in space if you're in the country. That's because cities have too much light, which makes stars and planets hard to see.

If Tara wants to see objects in space that are very far away, she can go to an observatory. This is a building that has the best tools for studying space, including powerful telescopes. Tara can't wait to learn more about telescopes. They make stargazing even more fun!

There are big observatories in space, such as the Hubble Space Telescope. It can see objects and events all over the universe!

# HISTORY OF TELESCOPES

| | |
|---|---|
| 1608 | Hans Lippershey designs the first refracting telescope. |
| 1609 | Galileo builds a refracting telescope to study space. |
| 1663 | James Gregory designs the first reflecting telescope. |
| 1688 | Sir Isaac Newton builds the first reflecting telescope. |
| 1840 | John William Draper takes the first close-up photograph of the moon using a telescope. |
| 1897 | The largest refracting telescope in the world is built for Yerkes Observatory in Wisconsin. |
| 1930 | Clyde Tombaugh discovers Pluto using a telescope at Lowell Observatory in Arizona. |
| 1990 | The Hubble Space Telescope is sent to space. |
| 2009 | The *Kepler* telescope is sent to space. |

# GLOSSARY

**constellation** (kahn-stuh-LAY-shun) A group of stars in the sky that is thought to look like an animal, object, or person.

**design** (dih-ZYN) A plan or outline showing how something is to be built.

**magnify** (MAAG-nuh-fy) To cause to appear larger.

**primary** (PRY-mehr-ee) Main.

**reflect** (rih-FLEHKT) To give back.

**source** (SOHRS) The start or cause of something.

**stargaze** (STAR-gayz) To look at or study the stars.

# INDEX